BLUE COLLAR JOBS ARE THE FUTURE

WHY YOU SHOULD LEARN A TRADE

Fitz Jr.

CONTENTS

Title Page

PREFACE

Request from the author

CHAPTER 1: Introduction   1

CHAPTER 2: Why Traditional College Degrees   4
May Not Be the Best Choice for Everyone

CHAPTER 3: The Benefits of Learning a Trade   7

CHAPTER 4: Dispelling the Myths About Blue   10
Collar Work

CHAPTER 5: The Evolving Image of Blue Collar   13
Workers

CHAPTER 6: The Growing Demand for Skilled   17
Tradespeople

CHAPTER 7: The High Cost of Student Debt and   20
the Advantages of Apprenticeships and On-The-Job
Traini

CHAPTER 8: The Role of Technology in the   23
Trades

CHAPTER 9: The Importance of Safety 27
Training and Workplace Regulations in Blue Collar
Jobs

CHAPTER 10: Exploring the Many Career Paths 31
in the Trades

CHAPTER 11: The Benefits of 35
Entrepreneurship and Small Business Ownership in
the Trades

CHAPTER 12: Breaking Down Barriers to Entry 39

CHAPTER 13: Conclusion 42

PREFACE

As I sit down to write this book, I can't help but reflect on my own personal journey. I hold a bachelor's degree, but throughout my career, I have always found myself gravitating toward jobs that require some sort of certification or license. This gave me the ability to find work almost anywhere and provided a level of job security that was hard to come by in other fields.

I vividly remember the day I decided to obtain my HVAC certification. At the time, I was working as a claims adjuster for the City of Jacksonville, and while I enjoyed my job, I knew deep down that I wanted more options. I wanted to learn a tangible skill that could help me not only personally but also professionally if I ever needed it. That's when I stumbled upon the HVAC industry and decided to take the leap and get certified.

Little did I know at the time that decision would have a profound impact on my life and how I viewed the job market. Not only did I learn a valuable skill that I could use in my personal life, but it also opened up a whole new world of career opportunities. I'm now able to work on HVAC systems in a variety of settings, from residential homes to large commercial buildings. And best of all, the demand for skilled HVAC technicians is high and will only increase as the current technicians become older and retire. That equals job security and competitive pay if I ever choose to do a career pivot.

This experience made me realize that there is so much potential in blue collar jobs and that learning a trade is a smart choice for anyone looking to build a successful career. In this book, I will share my insights and experiences on the changing landscape of the labor market, the benefits of learning a trade, and the various career paths and opportunities available in the trades. I hope this book inspires and empowers readers to consider the many advantages of blue collar work and encourages them to pursue a path that will lead to a fulfilling and financially secure career.

REQUEST FROM
THE AUTHOR

I kindly request that you leave a review on the book's page on Amazon. Your review will not only help potential readers make informed decisions, but it will also provide valuable feedback to the author.

CHAPTER 1:
INTRODUCTION

The Changing Landscape of the Labor Market

The world of work is constantly evolving, and nowhere is this more evident than in the labor market. In recent years, there has been a shift in the types of jobs that are in demand and a growing recognition of the value of blue collar work.

Traditionally, many people believed that a college degree was the key to a successful career. However, as the cost of higher education continues to rise and the job market becomes increasingly competitive, this belief is being called into question. While college degrees are still valuable in many fields, there is a growing demand for skilled tradespeople who can fill the gaps in industries such as construction, manufacturing, and transportation.

One reason for this shift is the changing nature of the economy. With the rise of automation and artificial intelligence, many jobs that were once considered "safe" are now at risk of being automated. This includes many white collar jobs, such as accounting and legal work, which can now be done more efficiently by computers. On the other hand, blue collar jobs, which often require physical labor and hands-on skills, are less likely to be replaced by machines.

Another factor contributing to the demand for blue collar workers is the aging of the workforce. As baby boomers retire, there are fewer skilled tradespeople to take their place. This has created a shortage of workers in fields such as plumbing, electrical work, and carpentry and has led to increased wages and job security for those who have the necessary skills.

Additionally, there is a growing recognition of the value of blue collar work. Many trades, such as welding and HVAC, require specialized skills that are in high demand. These skills cannot be learned in a classroom but must be acquired through hands-on training and experience. As a result, those who possess these skills are highly valued in the labor market and often enjoy competitive salaries and job stability.

Overall, the changing landscape of the labor market is creating new opportunities for those who are willing to learn a trade. While a college degree is still a valuable asset, it is no longer the only path to a successful career. In the chapters that follow, we will explore the benefits of blue collar work, the various career paths available in the trades, and the skills and certifications that are required to succeed in these fields.

CHAPTER 2: WHY TRADITIONAL COLLEGE DEGREES MAY NOT BE THE BEST CHOICE FOR EVERYONE

For many years, the path to a successful career has been seen as one that leads through college. Obtaining a bachelor's degree has been viewed as a necessary step toward achieving financial stability and professional success. However, the reality is that college may not be the best choice for everyone.

One reason for this is the rising cost of higher education. According to the College Board, the average cost of tuition and fees for the 2021-2022 academic year was $37,890 at private colleges and $10,560 for state residents at public colleges. This does not include additional expenses such as room and board, textbooks, and other supplies. The high cost of college has led many students to take out significant amounts of debt, which can take years, if not decades, to pay off.

Another issue is the oversaturation of certain fields. Many students choose to major in areas such as business, psychology, and communications, but there are often more graduates than there are job openings. This means that even with a degree, it can be difficult to find a job in these fields, and those who do often face stiff competition and lower salaries.

Furthermore, there is a growing recognition that a lot of people are not suited for a traditional college environment. Some individuals may struggle with academic coursework or may simply prefer hands-on learning to classroom instruction. For these individuals, learning a trade may be a better fit.

This is not to say that college is not valuable or important. In many fields, a degree is necessary to obtain certain positions, and college can provide a well-rounded education that is useful in a variety of settings. However, it is important to recognize that college may not be the best choice for everyone and that there are other paths to professional success.

In the chapters that follow, we will explore the benefits of learning a trade, the various career paths available in the trades, and the skills and certifications that are required to succeed in these fields. By understanding the full range of career options available, individuals can make informed decisions about their education and career paths and build successful and fulfilling careers.

CHAPTER 3: THE BENEFITS OF LEARNING A TRADE

Good Pay, Job Security, and Opportunities for Advancement

In recent years, there has been a growing recognition of the value of blue collar work, and the benefits that come with learning a trade. These benefits include good pay, job security, and opportunities for advancement.

Good Pay:

One of the most significant benefits of learning a trade is the potential for good pay. Many trades, such as welding, plumbing, and electrical work, offer competitive wages that can rival or even exceed those of some white collar professions.

In addition, many trades offer opportunities for overtime and bonuses, which can significantly increase earnings. For example, a skilled welder can earn a median annual wage of $42,490, while an experienced electrician can earn up to $94,620 per year.

Job Security:

Another advantage of learning a trade is job security. Many trades, such as HVAC technicians, carpenters, and automotive technicians, are in high demand and have low rates of unemployment. This is due in part to the aging of the workforce, as older tradespeople retire and create vacancies that need to be filled. In addition, many trades are less likely to be outsourced or automated, providing greater job security than some white collar professions. For example, as long as buildings need to be heated and cooled, there will always be a demand for HVAC technicians.

Opportunities For Advancement:

Finally, learning a trade can offer opportunities for advancement and career growth. Many trades offer apprenticeships or on-the-job training programs that provide individuals with the skills and knowledge they need to advance in their careers. In addition, many trades have a clear career path, with opportunities for promotion and increased responsibility. For example, electricians may start as apprentices but can eventually become journey workers or supervisors and may even start their own businesses.

Furthermore, trade work offers unique opportunities for those who enjoy working with their hands, solving problems, and taking pride in their work. Many tradespeople feel a sense of fulfillment from seeing the tangible results of their labor, such as a completed building, a repaired car, or a functioning HVAC system. This can lead to greater job satisfaction and a sense of purpose in one's work.

Overall, learning a trade can provide individuals with a path to financial stability, job security, and opportunities for advancement. In addition, trade work can provide a sense of fulfillment and purpose that may be lacking in some white collar professions. In the chapters that follow, we will explore the various trades and career paths available and the skills and certifications that are required to succeed in these fields. By understanding the benefits of learning a trade, individuals can make informed decisions about their education and career paths and build successful and fulfilling careers.

CHAPTER 4: DISPELLING THE MYTHS ABOUT BLUE COLLAR WORK

The Truth About Dirty Jobs

Despite the many benefits of learning a trade, there are still many myths and misconceptions about blue collar work that persist in society. One of the most pervasive of these myths is the idea that trade work is dirty, low-skill, and unfulfilling. In reality, however, many blue collar jobs are highly skilled, clean, and rewarding. In this chapter, we will dispel some of the common myths about dirty jobs and explain the truth about blue collar work.

Myth #1: Trade Work Is Dirty And Low-Skill

The first myth we need to address is the

idea that blue collar work is dirty and low-skill. While it is true that some trades, such as plumbing and automotive repair, may involve working with grease, oil, or other fluids, many trades do not. For example, electricians, carpenters, and HVAC technicians often work in clean and well-maintained environments. In addition, many trades require a high degree of skill and expertise, as well as ongoing education and training to stay current with the latest technologies and techniques.

Myth #2: Blue Collar Work Is Unfulfilling And Boring

Another common myth about trade work is that it is unfulfilling and boring. In reality, however, many trades offer opportunities for creativity, problem-solving, and critical thinking. For example, a carpenter may need to figure out how to fit a complex piece of trim into a tight space, while an HVAC technician may need to diagnose and repair a complex system. These challenges require ingenuity and resourcefulness and can provide a sense of fulfillment and accomplishment.

Myth #3: Trade Work Is Only For Men

Finally, there is a persistent myth that blue

collar work is only for men. While it is true that some trades, such as welding and construction, have traditionally been male-dominated, this is changing. Many trades, such as plumbing and electrical work, are now welcoming more women into the field. In addition, many trades are actively seeking to diversify their workforces and promote opportunities for women and minorities.

In conclusion, the idea that blue collar work is dirty, low-skill, and unfulfilling is a myth. Many trades offer clean and well-maintained work environments, as well as opportunities for creativity, problem-solving, and critical thinking. In addition, many trades are actively seeking to diversify their workforces and promote opportunities for women and minorities. By dispelling these myths and understanding the truth about blue collar work, individuals can make informed decisions about their education and career paths and build successful and fulfilling careers.

CHAPTER 5: THE EVOLVING IMAGE OF BLUE COLLAR WORKERS

From "Unskilled" Labor to Highly Skilled Professionals

For many years, blue collar workers were seen as unskilled laborers who performed dirty and physically demanding jobs. However, over time, the image of blue collar workers has evolved to reflect the highly skilled professionals that they are. In this chapter, we will explore the changing image of blue collar workers and the reasons behind this shift.

The Historical Image Of Blue Collar Workers

The image of blue collar workers as unskilled laborers can be traced back to the Industrial

Revolution when workers were often forced to perform repetitive and physically demanding tasks in factories and mines. These workers were paid low wages and had few opportunities for advancement or job security. As a result, blue collar work was often seen as a last resort for those who were unable to obtain white collar jobs.

The Shift To Highly Skilled Professionals

In recent years, however, the image of blue collar workers has shifted to reflect the highly skilled professionals that they are. This shift has been driven by a number of factors, including technological advancements, changes in the labor market, and a growing demand for skilled tradespeople.

Technological Advancements

One of the main drivers of the shift towards highly skilled blue collar workers has been technological advancements. As new technologies have been developed, many trades have become more complex and require a greater degree of skill and expertise to master. For example, the use of computerized machinery in manufacturing has led to a growing demand for workers who can operate and maintain these machines.

Changes In The Labor Market

Another factor driving the shift towards highly skilled blue collar workers has been changes in the labor market. With the decline of traditional manufacturing jobs and the growth of the service sector, there has been a growing demand for skilled tradespeople in industries such as construction, HVAC, and plumbing. As a result, these trades have become more competitive and require a higher level of skill and expertise to succeed.

A Growing Demand For Skilled Tradespeople

Finally, the shift towards highly skilled blue collar workers has been driven by a growing demand for these tradespeople. As the Baby Boomer generation retires, there is a shortage of skilled tradespeople to take their place. In addition, many young people are opting for traditional college degrees, leaving fewer people to pursue careers in the trades. As a result, tradespeople with specialized skills and expertise are in high demand and can command higher salaries and better job security.

In conclusion, the image of blue collar workers as unskilled laborers is outdated and inaccurate. Today's blue collar workers are highly skilled professionals who play a vital role in the economy. The shift towards highly skilled blue collar workers has been driven by technological advancements, changes in the labor market, and a growing demand for skilled tradespeople. By recognizing the value of blue collar work and the expertise required to succeed in these fields, individuals can make informed decisions about their education and career paths and build successful and fulfilling careers as highly skilled blue collar professionals.

CHAPTER 6: THE GROWING DEMAND FOR SKILLED TRADESPEOPLE

A Look at Industry Trends and Projections

As the economy continues to shift towards a knowledge-based economy, there is a growing demand for skilled tradespeople who can fill jobs in industries such as construction, manufacturing, and transportation. In this chapter, we will explore industry trends and projections for the demand for skilled tradespeople and the opportunities and benefits that come with pursuing a career in the trades.

Industry Trends And Projections

According to a report by the Bureau of Labor Statistics, many skilled trades are projected to experience job growth over the next decade. For example, the employment of plumbers, pipefitters, and steamfitters is projected to grow 14% from 2018 to 2028, faster than the average for all occupations. Similarly, employment of HVAC technicians is projected to grow 13% from 2018 to 2028. In addition, the report states that construction and extraction occupations are projected to add the most new jobs, with an estimated 864,800 new jobs added from 2018 to 2028.

In addition to job growth, many skilled trades also offer good pay and job security. According to the National Bureau of Economic Research, the median income for blue collar workers in the US is $23 per hour, which is higher than the median income for many white collar jobs. In addition, skilled tradespeople often have job security, as the demand for their services is unlikely to decline in the near future.

Opportunities And Benefits

Pursuing a career in the trades offers a number of opportunities and benefits. One of the main benefits is that tradespeople can learn practical, hands-on skills that are in high demand. Many trade schools and apprenticeships offer on-the-job training, which can provide valuable experience and help individuals build a strong foundation of skills and knowledge. In addition, tradespeople often have the opportunity to work on a variety of projects, which can keep the work interesting and challenging.

Another benefit of pursuing a career in the trades is that it can offer opportunities for advancement and entrepreneurship. Many tradespeople start out as apprentices or entry-level workers but can advance to higher-paying positions as they gain experience and develop their skills. In addition, tradespeople can start their own businesses and become entrepreneurs, which can offer greater flexibility and control over their work.

In conclusion, the growing demand for skilled tradespeople offers many opportunities for individuals who are interested in pursuing a career in the trades. With job growth projected in many industries, good pay, and opportunities for advancement and entrepreneurship, the trades can offer a fulfilling and financially rewarding career path. By recognizing the value of skilled trades and the opportunities they offer, individuals can make informed decisions about their education and career paths and build successful and fulfilling careers as skilled tradespeople.

CHAPTER 7: THE HIGH COST OF STUDENT DEBT AND THE ADVANTAGES OF APPRENTICESHIPS AND ON-THE-JOB TRAINING

As college tuition costs continue to rise, many students are left with significant student loan debt upon graduation. In this chapter, we will explore the high cost of student debt and the advantages of pursuing apprenticeships and on-the-job training as alternatives to a traditional college education.

The High Cost Of Student Debt

According to the Federal Reserve, the total outstanding student loan debt in the US reached $1.56 trillion in 2020, making it the second largest category of consumer debt after mortgages. The average student loan debt per borrower is $32,731, and many students struggle to pay off their loans, which can take decades to fully repay. The high cost of student debt can have significant long-term effects on a person's financial stability and ability to save for their future.

Advantages Of Apprenticeships And On-The-Job Training

One alternative to traditional college education is pursuing apprenticeships and on-the-job training. These programs offer a number of advantages, including the ability to learn practical, hands-on skills while earning a paycheck. Apprenticeships and on-the-job training programs often provide training that is specific to a particular trade and can offer individuals the opportunity to learn from experienced professionals in the field.

In addition, apprenticeships and on-the-job training programs can offer a pathway to a successful career without the burden of student loan debt. Many programs offer paid training, and as individuals gain experience and develop their skills, they can often earn higher wages and advance to higher-paying positions. According to the US Department of Labor, the average starting wage for an apprentice is $15 per hour, and wages increase as apprentices gain experience and complete their training.

Another advantage of pursuing apprenticeships and on-the-job training is that it can offer a direct pathway to a job. Many programs have partnerships with employers who are actively seeking skilled workers, and graduates of these programs often have an advantage when it comes to finding employment.

In conclusion, the high cost of student debt is a significant issue facing many college graduates, and it can have long-term effects on their financial stability and ability to save for their future. Apprenticeships and on-the-job training offer a viable alternative to traditional college education, providing individuals with practical, hands-on skills and a pathway to a successful career without the burden of student loan debt. By exploring the options available and considering apprenticeships and on-the-job training programs, individuals can make informed decisions about their education and career paths and build successful and financially stable futures.

CHAPTER 8: THE ROLE OF TECHNOLOGY IN THE TRADES

How Automation and Robotics Are Changing the Game

Advancements in technology have transformed nearly every aspect of modern life, including the world of trade work. In this chapter, we will explore the role of technology in the trades and how automation and robotics are changing the game.

Automation In The Trades

Automation refers to the use of technology to perform tasks that were previously done by humans. In the trades, automation has led to increased efficiency, accuracy, and safety.

For example, robotic arms can be used in manufacturing to perform tasks that were once done by human workers, such as welding or painting. This not only increases efficiency but also reduces the risk of injury to workers.

Another example of automation in the trades is the use of 3D printing technology. 3D printing allows for the creation of custom-made parts and tools, reducing the need for large inventories of pre-made parts. This technology has the potential to significantly reduce the cost of manufacturing and increase efficiency in the trades.

Robotics In The Trades

Robotics refers to the use of machines to perform tasks that were once done by humans. In the trades, robotics has led to the development of advanced machinery and equipment, such as automated CNC machines and robotic exoskeletons.

CNC machines, or computer numerical control machines, are used in manufacturing to create parts with high precision and accuracy. These machines use computer software to control the movements of the cutting tools, resulting in parts that are more accurate and consistent than those made by human workers.

Robotic exoskeletons are wearable devices that assist workers in performing physically demanding tasks, such as heavy lifting. These devices can reduce the risk of injury to workers and increase efficiency by allowing workers to perform tasks more quickly and with less effort.

The Future Of Technology In The Trades

As technology continues to advance, the role of automation and robotics in the trades will continue to grow. The use of artificial intelligence, or AI, is already being explored in the trades. AI could be used to analyze data from sensors and machines, leading to more efficient processes and reduced downtime.

In addition, virtual and augmented reality technology is being used in training programs for tradespeople. This technology allows individuals to simulate real-world scenarios and practice their skills in a safe and controlled environment.

In conclusion, technology has had a significant impact on the trades, with automation and robotics leading to increased efficiency, accuracy, and safety. As technology continues to advance, the role of automation and robotics in the trades will only continue to grow, leading to even greater efficiencies and innovations. By staying up-to-date on the latest technological advancements and learning new skills, tradespeople can remain competitive and succeed in a rapidly evolving industry.

CHAPTER 9: THE IMPORTANCE OF SAFETY TRAINING AND WORKPLACE REGULATIONS IN BLUE COLLAR JOBS

Safety is a top priority in any workplace, especially in blue-collar jobs where workers are often exposed to physical hazards and dangerous situations. In this chapter, we will explore the importance of safety training and workplace regulations in blue-collar jobs, as well as the growing demand for safety professionals in these industries.

The Importance Of Safety Training

Safety training is crucial in blue-collar jobs to prevent accidents and injuries. Workers must be trained on how to operate machinery and equipment safely, as well as how to identify and mitigate potential hazards in their work environment.

Employers are responsible for providing safety training to their workers, but it is also important for workers to take the initiative and seek out additional training opportunities. Many safety organizations offer training courses and certifications that can enhance a worker's skills and make them more competitive in the job market.

Workplace Regulations And Compliance

Workplace regulations are put in place to protect workers and ensure that employers are providing a safe and healthy work environment. These regulations vary by industry and are enforced by federal and state agencies.

Employers must comply with workplace regulations or face penalties and fines. Workers have the right to report safety violations without fear of retaliation, and employers are required to investigate and address any reported safety concerns.

Safety Position Job Opportunities

As the importance of safety in blue-collar jobs continues to grow, so does the demand for safety professionals. Safety engineers, coordinators, and inspectors are just a few examples of safety positions that are in high demand in blue-collar industries.

These positions require specialized training and certifications and often involve working closely with management and workers to ensure that safety standards are being met. Safety professionals can also play a key role in developing and implementing safety programs and policies.

In conclusion, safety training and workplace regulations are essential in blue-collar jobs to prevent accidents and injuries. Employers must provide their workers with proper safety training, and workers must take initiative to seek out additional training opportunities. Workplace regulations exist to protect workers and ensure that employers are providing a safe work environment. The growing demand for safety professionals in blue-collar industries highlights the importance of safety in these jobs and the opportunities available to those with specialized safety training and certifications.

CHAPTER 10: EXPLORING THE MANY CAREER PATHS IN THE TRADES

From Welders and Electricians to HVAC Technicians and Plumbers

The trades offer a wide range of career opportunities for those interested in working with their hands and pursuing a career that does not require a traditional four-year college degree. In this chapter, we will explore some of the most popular career paths in the trades, including welding, electrical work, HVAC technician, and plumbing.

Welders

Welders are responsible for joining pieces of metal together using heat and pressure. They may work on a variety of projects, from constructing buildings and bridges to fabricating machinery and equipment.

To become a welder, individuals typically need to complete a vocational training program or apprenticeship. They also need to be proficient in various welding techniques and familiar with safety procedures.

Electricians

Electricians install, maintain, and repair electrical systems in buildings and homes. They must have a strong understanding of electrical theory, as well as knowledge of safety procedures and regulations.

To become an electrician, individuals typically complete a vocational training program or apprenticeship. They may also need to pass a licensing exam and meet other state requirements.

Hvac Technicians

HVAC (heating, ventilation, and air conditioning) technicians are responsible for installing and maintaining HVAC systems in buildings and homes. They must have a strong understanding of heating and cooling systems, as well as knowledge of safety procedures and regulations.

To become an HVAC technician, individuals typically complete a vocational training program or apprenticeship. They may also need to pass a licensing exam and meet other state requirements.

Plumbers

Plumbers install and repair plumbing systems in buildings and homes. They may work on pipes, fixtures, and appliances, as well as perform maintenance and repair work.

To become a plumber, individuals typically complete a vocational training program or apprenticeship. They may also need to pass a licensing exam and meet other state requirements.

Other Trades

In addition to these popular trades, there are many other career paths in the trades, including carpentry, masonry, landscaping, and automotive repair. Each of these trades requires specialized knowledge and skills, as well as a commitment to safety and quality work.

In conclusion, the trades offer many career opportunities for those interested in pursuing a hands-on career that does not require a traditional four-year college degree. Welders, electricians, HVAC technicians, and plumbers are just a few examples of the many career paths available in the trades. Each of these trades requires specialized knowledge and skills, as well as a commitment to safety and quality work. By exploring the many career paths in the trades, individuals can find a career that fits their interests, skills, and goals.

CHAPTER 11:
THE BENEFITS OF ENTREPRENEURSHIP AND SMALL BUSINESS OWNERSHIP IN THE TRADES

Entrepreneurship and small business ownership in the trades can offer a range of benefits that are not always available to an employee. In this chapter, we will explore these benefits in more detail.

Freedom And Flexibility

Entrepreneurship and small business ownership provide individuals with the freedom and flexibility to choose their own work schedule and workload. As a business owner, they have the ability to set their own hours, determine their own projects and clients, and decide the pace of their work. This allows them to balance their work with other important aspects of their lives, such as family, hobbies, and other personal pursuits.

Income Potential

Entrepreneurship and small business ownership also offer the potential for higher income compared to working as an employee in the trades. As business owners, individuals have the ability to set their own rates and charge what they believe their services are worth. They also have the ability to take on more clients and increase their revenue, thereby increasing their earning potential.

Creative Control

Entrepreneurship and small business ownership in the trades also provide individuals with the ability to exercise creative control over their work. As business owners, they can develop their own brand and unique style and have the freedom to introduce innovative services and products to the market. This allows them to differentiate themselves from other businesses and appeal to a broader range of clients.

Job Security

Entrepreneurship and small business ownership also offer a level of job security that may not always be available as an employee in the trades. By owning their own business, individuals can diversify their services and products, as well as their client base. This can help to insulate them from changes in the market and economic downturns, providing them with a more secure source of income.

Challenges And Considerations

Entrepreneurship and small business ownership in the trades also come with their own set of challenges and considerations. Starting and running a successful business requires a significant amount of time, effort, and resources. This includes financial investment, the ability to manage and delegate tasks effectively, and the need to continually market and grow the business.

In conclusion, entrepreneurship and small business ownership in the trades can provide individuals with the freedom, income potential, creative control, and job security that may not always be available as an employee. However, starting and running a successful business requires a significant amount of hard work, dedication, and investment. Individuals interested in pursuing this path should carefully consider the pros and cons and ensure they have the necessary skills, resources, and mindset to succeed. With the right preparation and commitment, entrepreneurship and small business ownership in the trades can be a rewarding and fulfilling career path.

CHAPTER 12: BREAKING DOWN BARRIERS TO ENTRY

How to Get Started in the Trades and Build a Successful Career

For many people, the idea of entering a trade can seem daunting. They may not know where to start, what kind of training they need, or how to find job opportunities. However, with the right guidance and resources, anyone can build a successful career in the trades.

One of the first steps to getting started in the trades is to do some research and figure out which area interests you the most. There are many different trades to choose from, including welding, plumbing, electrical work, carpentry, and more. Each of these trades has its own set of skills, training requirements, and career paths.

Once you have identified the trade you want to pursue, the next step is to get the necessary training and certification. Many community colleges, trade schools, and vocational schools offer programs that teach the skills and knowledge needed to work in the trades. These programs can range from a few weeks to a few years in length, depending on the trade and level of certification.

In addition to formal training programs, apprenticeships, and on-the-job training can also provide valuable experience and knowledge. Apprenticeships allow individuals to learn from experienced tradespeople while earning a wage and often lead to full-time employment after completion.

Another important aspect of building a successful career in the trades is networking and building relationships with other professionals in the industry. Joining trade organizations, attending industry events, and connecting with others through social media can all help expand your network and lead to job opportunities.

It is also important to stay up-to-date with the latest trends and technologies in your trade. Continuously learning and adapting to new techniques and tools can make you a more valuable employee and help you advance in your career.

Breaking down barriers to entry in the trades also means addressing issues of diversity and inclusion. Historically, the trades have been male-dominated, but efforts are being made to encourage more women and people of color to pursue careers in the trades. Programs and initiatives aimed at promoting diversity and inclusion can help create a more inclusive and equitable industry.

Finally, it is important to prioritize safety in the trades. Many trades involve working with dangerous equipment or in hazardous environments, so proper safety training and precautions are essential. Employers should provide a safe working environment, and employees should take responsibility for following safety protocols and reporting any potential hazards.

In conclusion, getting started in the trades can seem overwhelming, but with the right preparation, training, and networking, anyone can build a successful career in this field. By breaking down barriers to entry, promoting diversity and inclusion, and prioritizing safety, the trades can provide a fulfilling and lucrative career path for individuals of all backgrounds and skill levels.

CHAPTER 13: CONCLUSION

In conclusion, blue collar jobs are the backbone of the economy and will continue to be so in the future. As technology advances, it is becoming clear that many of these jobs are highly skilled, require technical knowledge, and offer competitive wages and benefits. Additionally, many blue-collar jobs offer opportunities for advancement, entrepreneurship, and small business ownership.

It is important to dispel the myths and misconceptions about blue collar work and recognize the many benefits of pursuing a career in the trades. Whether you are a recent high school graduate, a college graduate looking for a career change, or simply seeking a path to financial stability, the trades offer a wide range of opportunities for growth and success.

Furthermore, the demand for skilled tradespeople is on the rise and is projected to continue growing in the coming years. With the high cost of college and student debt, pursuing a career in the trades through apprenticeships and on-the-job training can be a smart financial decision.

It is also crucial to note the importance of safety training and workplace regulations in blue collar jobs. Workplace safety should always be a top priority to ensure the well-being of workers and prevent accidents.

In conclusion, the future of work is changing, and blue collar jobs are becoming more important than ever. By breaking down barriers to entry and providing opportunities for growth and success, the trades can offer a fulfilling and financially rewarding career path for anyone willing to work hard and develop their skills.

Made in the USA
Monee, IL
16 October 2024

68101236R00030